Tate Gallery
St Ives
The Building

Evans and Shalev Architects

**Edited by David Shalev
and Michael Tooby**

Tate Publishing

Contents

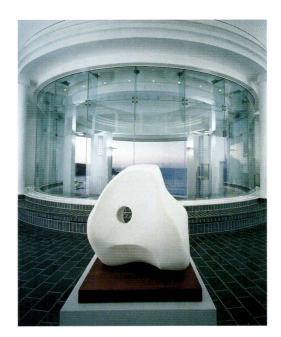

Introduction
David Hamilton Eddy

In 1920 Bernard Leach and Shoji Hamada came to St Ives, Cornwall, to found the only outpost of *raku* or 'rough' ceramics outside Japan. *Raku* inspires the bowls used in the traditional tea ceremony. In 1928 Ben Nicholson and Christopher Wood, modernist artists, were moved to paint in a new way by seeing the 'naive' pictures of the St Ives painter Alfred Wallis.

After the outbreak of war in 1939, Ben Nicholson, Barbara Hepworth and the Russian Constructivist Naum Gabo arrived in St Ives at the invitation of Adrian Stokes, the painter, poet and writer and his first wife, the artist Margaret Mellis. The threesome variously dedicated their work to investigating Cubism, archetypal images of early cultures and to exploring the essential nature of materials, whether traditional wood, stone and bronze or modern ones like plastic and alloy.

In 1945, a third wave of artists following the same modernist agenda, Wilhelmina Barns-Graham, John Wells, Sven Berlin, Peter Lanyon (the only native Cornishman), Bryan Wynter and Terry Frost, drifted to St Ives. The Crypt Group – which later evolved into Penwith Society of Arts – was a modernist cabal seen as fiercely hostile to the traditional British Impressionistic St Ives school of painting. At the time of the Festival of Britain in 1951, St Ives painters and sculptors – influentially linked to British architecture through Leslie Martin, co-founder of the 1930 arts magazine *Circle* with Nicholson and Gabo – dominated the English modernist art scene.

At the time of the death of Barbara Hepworth much of the work of these artists was in the collection of the Tate Gallery in

Tate Gallery St Ives viewed from Man's Head (*above*)

Morley Easthorne working on the foundation stone (*left*)

The Tate Gallery and Porthmeor Beach (*opposite*)

London where for many years it was stored in the basement. However, encouraged by the successful precedents of the Tate's Barbara Hepworth Museum in St Ives and by James Stirling's Tate Gallery in Liverpool, a new museum project, Tate Gallery St Ives was mooted and thanks to the passionate lobbying of associations like the St Ives Tate Action Group, sufficient money was raised locally, nationally and through the EC (whose grant covered more than half of the £3.5 million cost of the new building).

The architects of the new Tate Gallery St Ives, opened by HRH The Prince of Wales on 23 June 1993, were Eldred Evans and David Shalev, designers of the award-winning and highly respected County Court House in Truro. Evans and Shalev have lived in St Ives for many years. The building stems from the same modernist search for naturalness and honesty of materials that inspired Leach, Hamada, Nicholson, Hepworth and Gabo. Its exterior rough pebbledash finish reflects the fishermen's cottages it is set among. But the interior, smooth, white and pure, beautifully lit by natural light, induces a serenity crucial to the meditational mood we need for the appreciation of works of art.

In this sense, Tate Gallery St Ives is of Le Corbusier's intuitive or organic modernism rather than Mies van der Rohe's rationalistic cubes on stilts, despite the fact that essentially the building is composed of cool, static cubes invaded by the dynamic cylinders of the main entrance rotunda and the minor circular exhibition space, linked to the major by an internal mall which is flooded by mauve light from Patrick Heron's stained-glass window. The cubes and cylinders reflect Nicholson's Cubist interests and this theme is reprised in the circular and rectilinear windows. But the disposition of spaces is so gracefully

achieved that negotiating the building encourages the same relaxed pleasure one gets from exploring the curving lanes of St Ives itself.

Thus, the simplicity and strength of the overall conception only intensifies the vivid pleasure of the beautifully detailed natural ash balustrade, the stone-floored restaurant with its elegant trapezium plan floating above the gardens and cottages around, the gorgeous ceramic gallery overlooking the main entrance and the noble proportions and still ambience of the main galleries.

Here it is very much worth noting that all the emphasis is on the works of art and not on the 'architecture': much museum architecture in recent years has been a more or less unconscious competition between artist and architect.

Evans and Shalev's ability to make sympathetic architecture stems from their capacity to 'make a journey into the unknown'. The confidence to do that is based on their mastery of the basics: 'In the

past, there were masters – Corb, Mies, Aalto, Wright. Everybody then talked the same language, it gave you a basis to develop from. Today, architecture follows literary theory, deconstruction – which is anti-form. Everything has become very introverted, detached from the continuity of history.'

Shalev and Evans both agree that one cannot draw spaces, they have to be built, and it is impossible to anticipate what they will look like. In the end, by obeying the rules of that Eastern reticence that Leach and Hamada obeyed, Evans and Shalev achieve great architecture. These rules are not written down nor will they ever be, but they are to do with harmony, *wa* in Japanese. The building is in harmony with the people who built it, with the people who will use it, in harmony with the little town, in harmony, finally with the big wide sea that stretches to the Americas, to that New World which the modernist artists of St Ives wanted to reach.

Influences

Tate Gallery St Ives was designed to show works of art in the place in which they were and will be created. It relates to the works it exhibits in that both are often inspired by St Ives and the surrounding landscape. The art, the building, the townscape and landscape form part of one experience.

Stepped alley in St Ives (*far left*)
St Ives seen from Barnoon Hill (*left*)
St Ives harbour at low tide (*above*)
Nanjizel, west Cornwall (*right*)

Rocks at Rosewall Hill, near St Ives (*above*)
Men-an-tol, near Morvah, Cornwall (*left*)
The Cornish coastline (*right*)

W. S. Graham's work reflected his close ties with his artist friends. Graham, a Scot, lived at Madron and was particularly associated with Roger Hilton, Bryan Wynter, Peter Lanyon and Karl Weschke. Graham joined them in admiring the work of Alfred Wallis.

Alfred Wallis, 'Schooner under the Moon' *c.*1935–6

This picture was framed by Adrian Stokes to show a lozenge-shaped board, with the horizon level, as reproduced here. Wallis made many works which actually showed a 'sloping' sea, evoking a heavy swell which is climbed by a ship. In the Gallery the work is therefore hung with the bottom edge of the board itself parallel to the floor, so that the ship rises to the left.

The Constructed Space
W. S. Graham

Meanwhile surely there must be something to say,
Maybe not suitable but at least happy
In a sense here between us two whoever
We are. Anyhow here we are and never
Before have we two faced each other who face
Each other now across this abstract scene
Stretching between us. This is a public place
Achieved against subjective odds and then
Mainly an obstacle to what I mean.

It is like that, remember. It is like that
Very often at the beginning till we are met
By some intention risen up out of nothing.
And even then we know what we are saying
Only when it is said and fixed and dead.
Or maybe, surely, of course we never know
What we have said, what lonely meanings are read
Into the space we make. And yet I say
This silence here for in it I might hear you.

I say this silence or, better, construct this space
So that somehow something may move across
The caught habits of language to you and me.
From where we are it is not us we see
And times are hastening yet, disguise is mortal.
The times continually disclose our home.
Here in the present tense disguise is mortal.
The trying times are hastening. Yet here I am
More truly now in this abstract art become.

Evans and Shalev knew the artists' community
of St Ives long before the idea of Tate Gallery
St Ives was discussed. Eldred Evans's father,
Merlyn Evans, had a studio in the town from
1962. The family continue to use it as a base in
Cornwall. The light and space of the different
studios, and associated memories of the
differing personalities of the artists, informed
their designs.

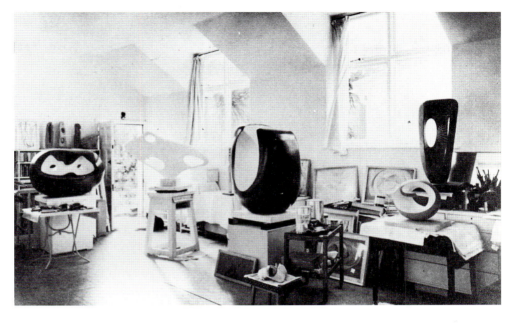

Barbara Hepworth's Trewyn Studio, 1959
(*top*)

Ben Nicholson in his studio, St Ives
*c.*1949–51 (*bottom*)

Barbara Hepworth, 'Two Figures (Menhirs)' 1964 (*left*)

Ben Nicholson, 'Feb 28–53 (vertical seconds)' 1953 (*right*)

Bernard Leach, 'Tile' *c*.1925. Wingfield Digby Collection (*far right, top*)

Shoji Hamada, 'Vase' 1930s. Wingfield Digby Collection (*far right, bottom*)

The work of Bernard Leach and his pottery has had an enormous influence on the character of St Ives art. The Tate Gallery's usual collection and display policy was extended in St Ives to include the showing of pots alongside painting and sculpture.

The upper level of gallery 2 was conceived by the architects as an area where a range of ceramics could be displayed in the heart of the building yet with its own distinct space and character.

The Site

The Gallery occupies a formerly derelict, steeply falling north-facing site, on which the town gasworks once stood. The building overlooks Porthmeor Beach and commands views over the town's rooftops and harbour out to St Ives Bay, with a panorama that extends westwards to Clodgy Point and eastwards to Godrevy Lighthouse.

View from the Gallery looking over the town to The Island (*above*)

The gasworks, Porthmeor Beach, *c.*1963 (*left, above*)

Commencing work on the site, June 1991 (*left*)

The Design Concept
Evans and Shalev

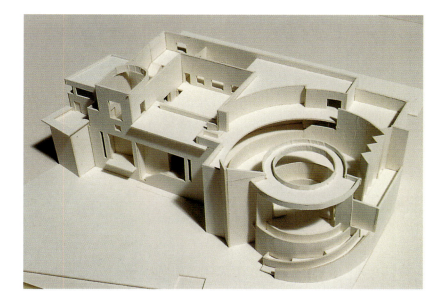

The design concept of the Gallery was formed in late 1989 as a response to a single stage Architectural Competition Brief, compiled by Cornwall County Council.

There has always been a connection between nature, art and architecture. All and each can evoke deep feelings. Nature is transformed in art and architecture. The transformation is in the creative act in which the artist invents his belief and faith.

Architecture at its best is inseparable from both the visual and performing arts. Good architecture is also by its very nature a manifestation of a way of life. This is why designing for art is a profound experience. It also explains why good architecture always belongs, relates, connects and is 'part of'.

St Ives is unique in that its architecture, landscape and art are so closely interwoven. The Penwith peninsula evokes a sense of history – the relationship between Man and Nature, us and the elements, is ever present. It is this experience that attracts artists to Penwith. It is the same experience that we tried to capture in our building.

In architecture the built form contains a space. This space has certain dimensions, proportions, texture, light, colour and sound. This space also opens to another space or to the outside world. It is the interplay between these elements, the juxtaposition of spaces and the sequential perception in moving through them that creates the experience of architecture. It is an experience in time, akin to music, dance and poetry and unlike painting and sculpture.

In designing spaces for and around art, all forms of art and craft, it is imperative that experiencing the architecture and experiencing the art are at best mutually informative and instructive, always complementary and never mutually exclusive. An art gallery is a place for seeing, listening and contemplating, which enables art to communicate, challenge, provoke, stimulate and inspire.

We see Tate Gallery St Ives both as home for past and present artists of St Ives and as catalyst for the future generation of artists.

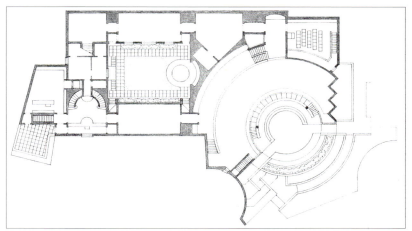

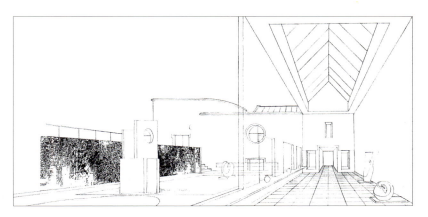

Illustrations on pp.15–19 were included in the competition submission. (*From top*): early model of the Gallery; early plan of the main exhibition level; montage of the sculpture courtyard and gallery 4

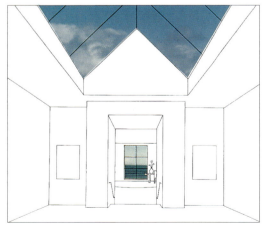

Alfred Wallis, 'St Ives' *c.*1928 (*above*)

Montage of the sky and sea, glimpsed through windows (*left*)

Artist's impression of the Gallery by Thomas Wan (*above*). A number of features were altered in the final design

Ben Nicholson, 'Porthmeor, Window Looking Out to Sea' 1930, Private Collection (*right*). The architects enjoyed the idea that visitors might associate the views from the Gallery windows with works such as this

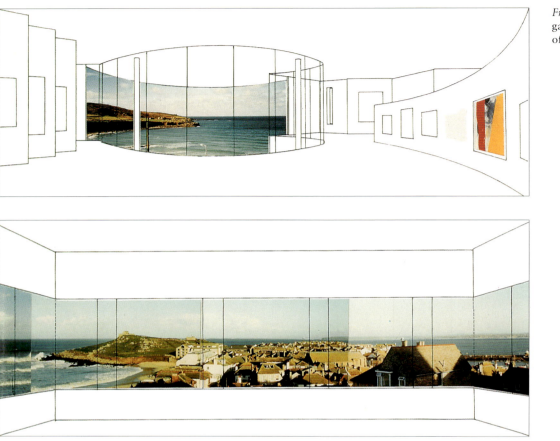

From top: montages of the view from gallery 2, of the view from the restaurant, and of Porthmeor Beach with the Gallery

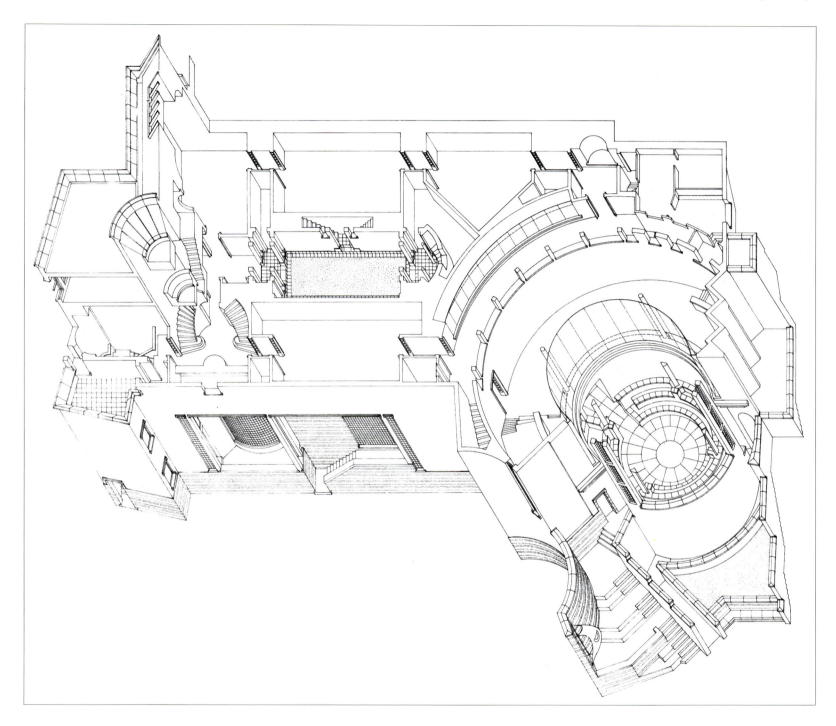

Axonometric plan of the Gallery

Construction

The Gallery, comprising a total floor area of approximately 1600m², is designed as a modern building incorporating up-to-date and forward-looking technology.

The building is constructed of a concrete and masonry frame, finished with white marble dash render, painted precast concrete cills, lintels and cornices, roof slating and reconstructed stone pavings. Windows are generally of painted wood, fully reversible for cleaning, a curved structural glass wall to the sculpture gallery, and sand-blasted glass blocks. The interior finishes are silent rubber flooring in the painting galleries and rustic slate flooring in the sculpture gallery and intermediate spaces. Walls are of white painted MDF boarding. The ceilings are moulded woodwork and generally house the air-conditioning and lighting facilities.

The environmental services are designed both to create a pleasant ambience throughout the year and to protect and preserve the works of art in fully air-conditioned rooms with automatic temperature and humidity controls and adjustable daylight control. The artificial lighting is designed to create a soft background lighting with flexible supplementary local lights.

The building was constructed and fitted over a period of two years from June 1991 to June 1993.

The building's construction was determined by the need to build the entire elevation sideways. A retaining wall was built against the cliff, then as the derelict and polluted site was cleared, the builders had to progress until the building eventually occupied the whole site.

Under construction: an aerial view of the Gallery (*left*); the loggia roof (*top right*); the back wall of gallery 2 (*right*)

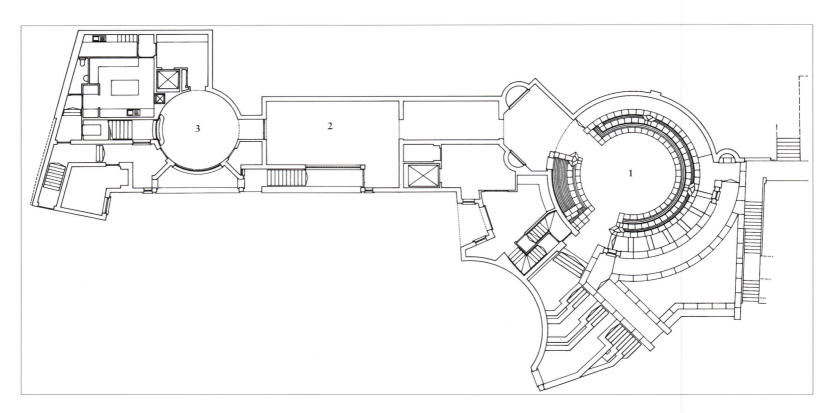

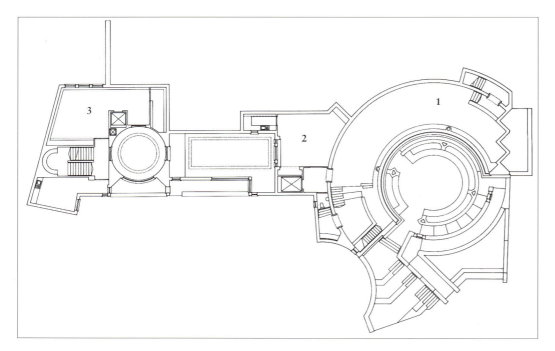

Ground floor plan (*top*):
1 loggia; 2 mall; 3 entrance to galleries

First floor plan (*left*):
1 sculpture gallery (gallery 2); 2 education room;
3 bookshop

Under construction: the Gallery viewed from the
west (*above*)

Second floor plan (*top right*):
1–5 galleries 1–5; 6 entrance to galleries;
7 courtyard; 8 curator's suite

Roof plan (*bottom right*):
1 restaurant; 2 roof terrace

Under construction: the restaurant windows
(*below*); the main stairs window (*bottom left*)

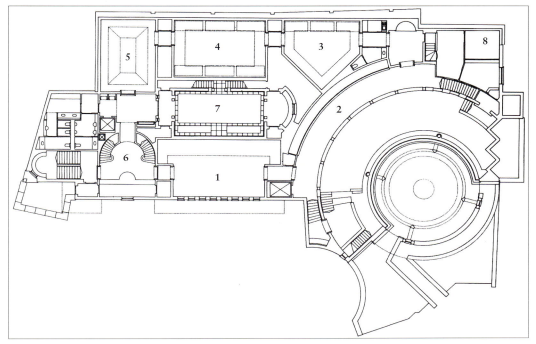

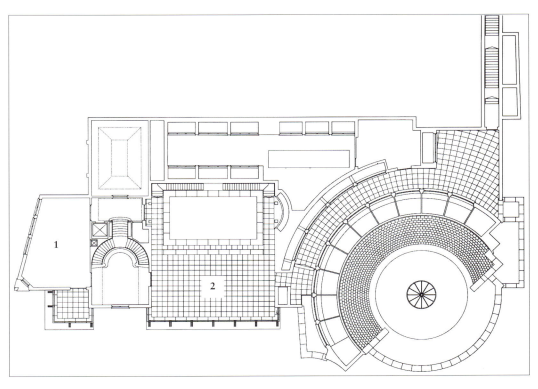

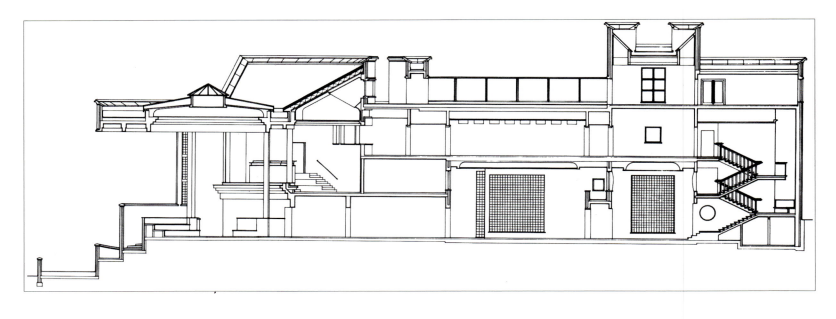

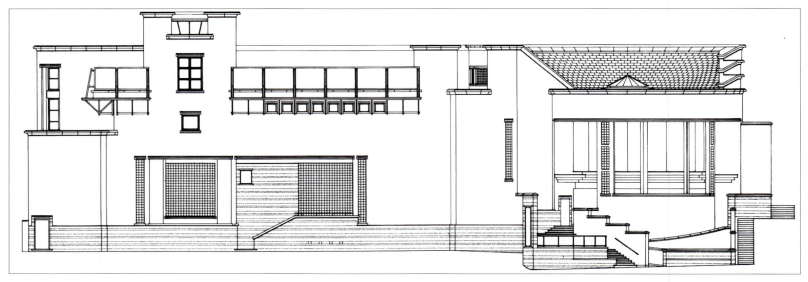

Longitudinal section through the loggia and main stairs (*top*)

North elevation facing Porthmeor Beach (*above*)

East and west elevations (*right*), showing how steeply the site slopes

Under construction: the courtyard (*far right, top*), and gallery 4 (*bottom*)

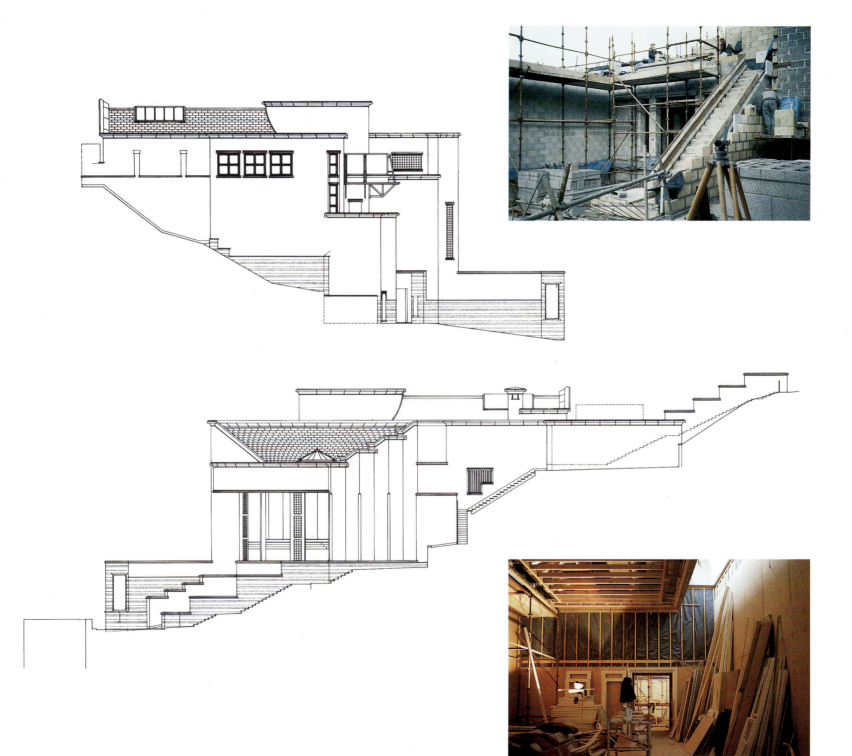

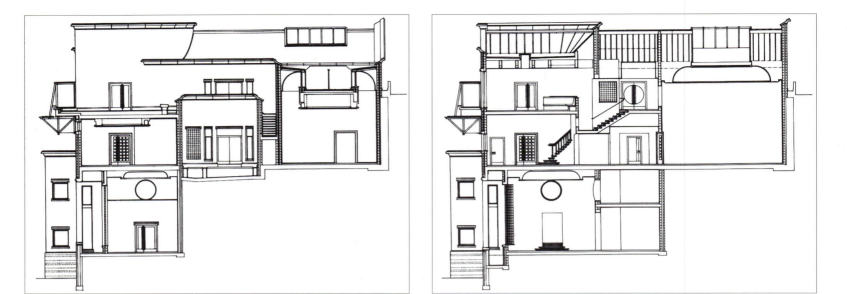

Sections through the Gallery, again showing how it is built into the cliffside (*above left and right*). The Gallery has only a small floor area on its lower floor. As the building rises, the floor area greatly increases

Under construction: reception and stairs to the restaurant (*left*)

Completing the approach steps (*right*)

A Tour through the Gallery

The Gallery, designed on four floors and comprising a number of studio-like daylit rooms, is perched on top of a sheer wall facing the bay. The sheltered undercroft is for the use of the town and provides space for theatrical, musical and other cultural events.

The progression from street to building and from building to street is very gradual. The approach spaces belong to both. The Gallery is a showcase, as galleries are, but being part of St Ives it is intended to become a hub of cultural and social activity.

The building is entered from below. The approach to the entrance from Beach Road is via the loggia: a small amphitheatrical space, which forms, once in the building, the window to the Atlantic. The main gallery area is located on the second floor, where it occupies the entire length and breadth of the site. Five top-lit exhibition rooms are arranged in a simple sequence around a secret courtyard – which is discovered at the end of the journey. Once on the main gallery level, the visitor follows a route through rooms of differing scale, proportions and light. The rooms

are no larger than those of a St Ives artist's studio. Sparse in detail with silent floors and softly lit, the spaces allow the exhibitions to come into their own.

The intention was to create spaces, with varying shapes, sizes and quality of light, receding to highlight the paintings and objects and create a relaxed atmosphere conducive to experiencing the art. Four of the rooms are for paintings, each with its own distinct character. The second gallery, circular and hugging the loggia, is predominantly for sculptures and ceramics – overlooking the sea, it is the window of the building.

The first low and elongated space lends itself to an introduction to the St Ives School. The bay is rediscovered from the circular space. Brightly lit, this largest space in the building houses sculpture by artists such as Barbara Hepworth, Naum Gabo and Denis Mitchell, with ceramic work by Bernard Leach and his school along the curved balcony. From here the route continues through the three main painting rooms with ever-increasing height and light, showing works by painters such as Ben Nicholson, Bryan Wynter, Peter Lanyon, Alfred Wallis and Patrick Heron.

Flexibility in use is achieved, not by creating an endlessly flexible anonymous structure, but by designing a set of unique rooms. The doorways between the rooms are small pause or transition spaces. The interior spaces are urban-like and echo the spaces of St Ives. The galleries are private and serene. Other spaces are open to capture the seascape and roofscape ever present in the building and the art.

An important part of an art gallery is the

facility to introduce children to the art world. To this end a small work/demonstration room is located en route, integrated but discrete. A bookshop is located on the way in or out.

On the roof of the Gallery is the restaurant. It is placed and designed to command a panoramic view of St Ives Bay – extending over the rooftops of the town and its harbour, out to sea, along the horizon from Clodgy Point to the Godrevy Lighthouse.

The exterior reflects the scale and texture of the town, and stands up to exposure to the ocean and the bay. St Ives is a town of white walls, grey slate roofs and small windows; so is the new building. The experience of visiting the Gallery is a natural extension to visiting St Ives and thus provides some insight into the artists' inspirations and aspirations on this remote and magical peninsular.

The Gallery on Porthmeor Beach (*left*)

The loggia ceiling (*above*)

A glimpse into the loggia (*right*)

The main approach (*left*)

Views of the loggia.
The sculpture on display is
'Willendorf Knot' 1991 by
Peter Randall-Page.
Collection of the Artist

The mall, with Patrick Heron's 'Window for Tate Gallery St Ives' 1992–3 in coloured glass (*opposite*). Heron did not want leaded lines separating the colours, and this is probably the largest coloured glass window in the world without leading. The German manufacturers worked with Heron to devise a way of cutting the glass in panels to reproduce the irregular boundaries of the colours in Heron's original design, which was a small gouache painting on paper. The natural irregularities in the handmade glass add another element to the original design

For the opening of the Gallery, Terry Frost made a banner for the main stairwell (*this page*). Frost's design used one of the artist's current motifs, the spiral, which he saw as appropriately celebratory and international in its resonances

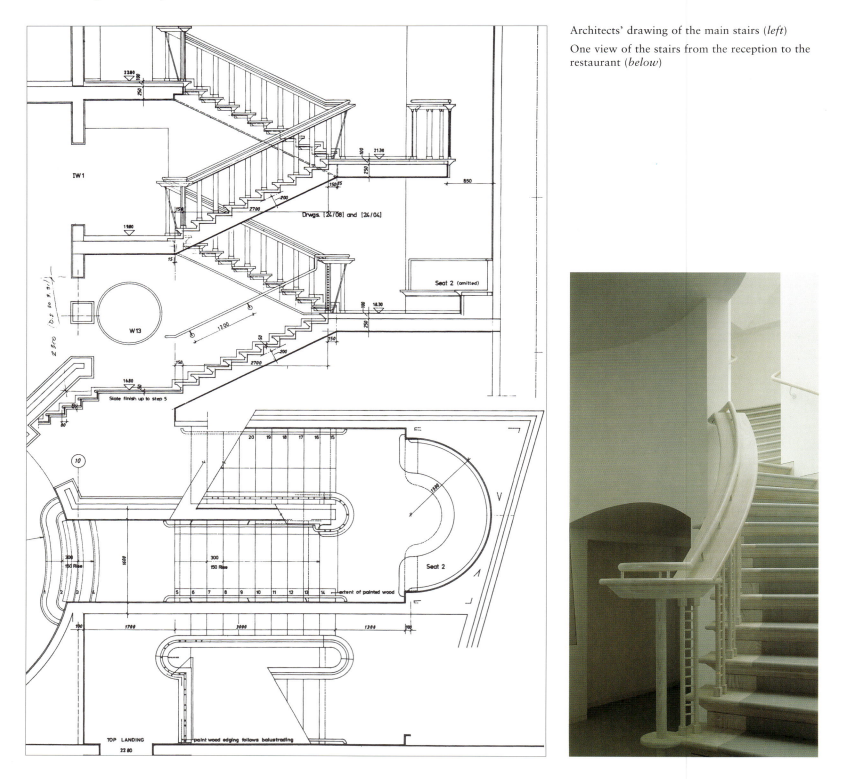

Architects' drawing of the main stairs (*left*)

One view of the stairs from the reception to the restaurant (*below*)

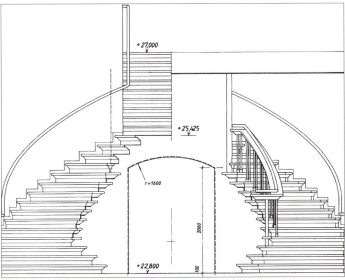

The stairs from the reception to the restaurant: architects' drawing and the stairs completed

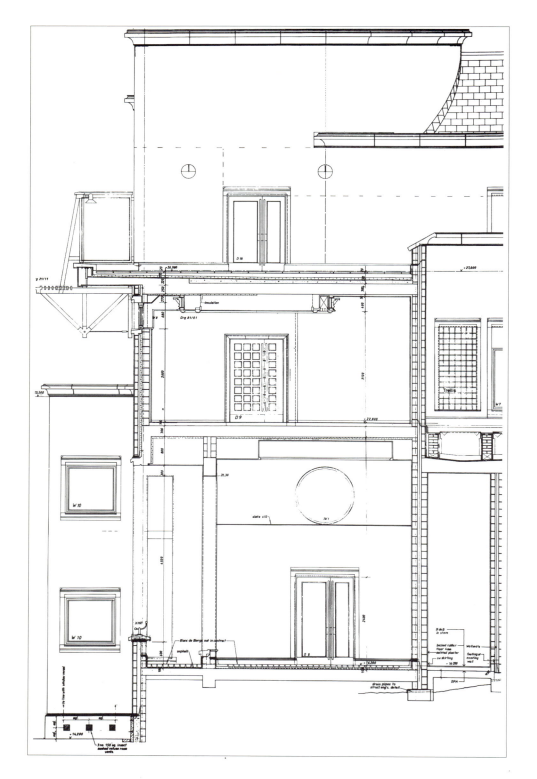

Section of the mall, gallery 1, and the roof terrace (*far left*)

Displays in gallery 2 (*left and bottom right*)

The pottery cabinet in gallery 2 (*top right*). This is lit both artificially and naturally from concealed windows high above

Gallery 2, viewed from two directions.

Views in gallery 2 (*above and opposite*). The window, which was made in sections and bolted together, is believed to be the largest bent structural glass window in the world. Glass fins, which protrude outwards to maintain an internal simplicity, strengthen the window

Porthmeor Beach seen from the window (unfinished) of gallery 2 (*left*).

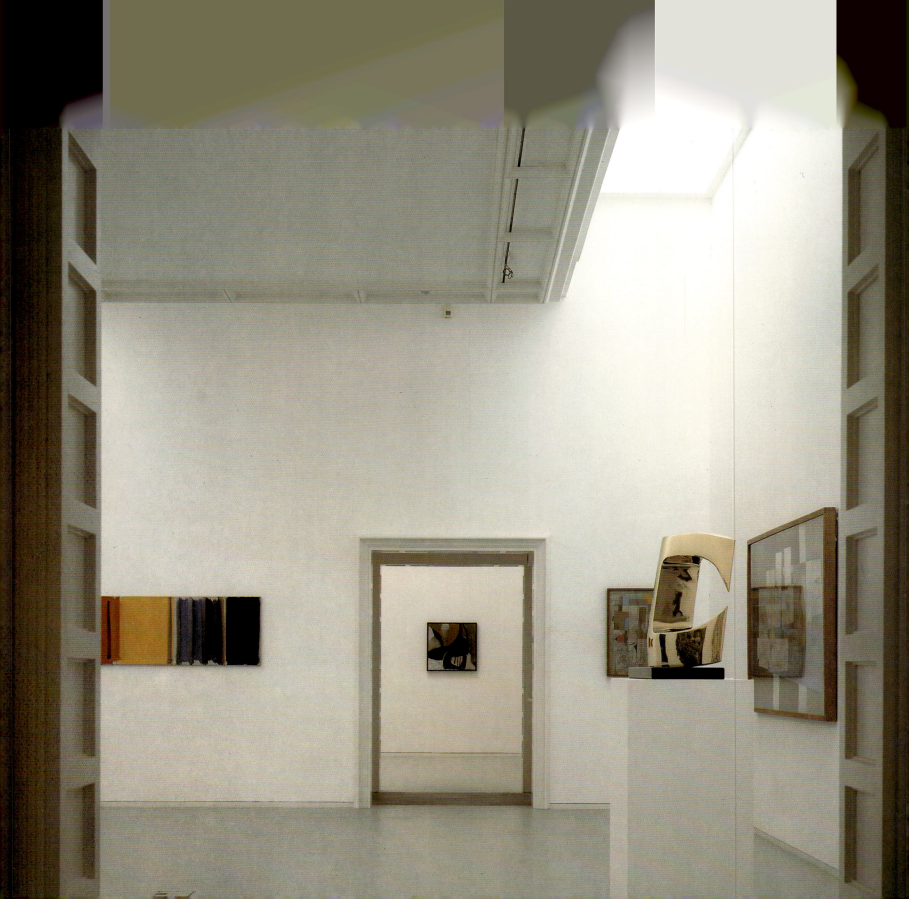

Gallery 4, looking through to gallery 5 (*left*). The doorways are placed off-centre to maximise useful hanging space

Gallery 3, looking through to gallery 4 and gallery 5 beyond (*right*), with the transition spaces in the doorways between rooms

The restaurant balcony (*top left*)

View from the roof terrace, looking toward The Island (*left*)

Stairs from the courtyard to the roof terrace (*above*)

View through a restaurant window (*opposite*)

Views on departure (*this page*)
The education studio (*opposite*)

The Building in Use

The experience of visiting Tate Gallery St Ives is often compared with the experience of visiting the town itself. At quiet times, one can wander leisurely round the Gallery, enjoying the relationship between its interior spaces and external location. The special character of the building shapes the visitor's progress: the rhythm of passage is broken by contrasting spaces, with possible routes hinted at by internal views and glimpses outside to various landmarks.

In the dedicated gallery spaces, each room prompts a different approach to the installation of works of art. Each ensemble of pieces, in the different installations encouraged by the architecture, can be considered carefully, whether individually, within small groupings or as part of the overall display.

The Gallery, like St Ives itself, is extraordinarily popular. In its busy times, the building comes alive with people strolling through, catching their breath at particular points, often returning to places or works first passed briefly to savour them at greater leisure or to give them deeper thought. Part of the atmosphere of the Gallery is how it gives breathing spaces in these moments when people can emerge from the crowded spaces onto large terraces, and turn from the works of art to the landscape.

The curatorial and educational approach to Gallery activities also took its initial cues from the direction created by the building itself. It provides direct personal contact, with a range of viewpoints. The diverse backgrounds of the Gallery staff themselves are brought to bear, alongside the different perspectives and experiences of a wide range of specialists, from artists and writers, to teachers, academics, those with practical skills to share, and even designers and architects.

These people produce in the building an atmosphere of creative work which is shared with the audiences attracted by their ideas and initiatives. The Gallery's educational work begins in the education studio, but often encompasses the entire building. From early in the morning to mid-afternoon, groups of children energise the whole Gallery. During the day adults from a variety of backgrounds use classes and workshops to develop their skills and extend their understanding, and in the evenings there are social events, lectures and debates.

For most visitors, the first direct personal contact with the staff and the educational role is through a daily guided tour. This usually begins in front of the window by Patrick Heron. In this space many of the threads between the building's design and the works of art become entwined. The visitor can stand in front of a space flooded with light of the extraordinary colour of Heron's window. They have already looked up into the gallery in the two-level curved space. They can look ahead and see glimpses of the passage through the building as if they were trying to guess what lay down a narrow St Ives alley. They will be overlooked by those distracted from their activity in the education studio, as paint-covered hands press against the window looking down on their group. Taking all this in, the group then begins to explore the works of art themselves.

Tate Gallery St Ives, viewed from The Island (*left*)

Contents page illustration Barbara Hepworth's 'Image II' 1960, displayed in gallery 2

Photo credits

Unless otherwise stated, photography is by the architects Evans and Shalev, or by Marcus Leith of Tate Gallery Photographic Department.

Bob Berry: pp.1, 8 (*top*), 9

Richard Bryant: pp.34 (*right*), 39, 42, 48

Roger Harvey ABIPP: back cover, pp.2, 4 (*bottom*), 7 (*bottom*), 20, 27, 29 (*top*); 33

John Edward Linden: front cover, pp.3, 5, 28, 30, 32, 35 (*top*), 38, 40 (*bottom*), 41

St Ives Times and Echo: p.14 (*top left*)

Studio St Ives: p.11 (*top*)

ISBN 1 85437 161 4

Published by Tate Publishing, Millbank, London SW1P 4RG

© Tate Gallery 1995

Designed by James Shurmer

Printed in Italy by Amilcare Pizzi, Milan